GO TURBO

FORMULA 1

TOM PALMER

EDGE FRANKLIN WATTS

LONDON·SYDNEY

First published in 2009 by
Franklin Watts
338 Euston Road
London NW1 3BH

Franklin Watts Australia
Level 17/207 Kent Street
Sydney NSW 2000

Series editor: Adrian Cole
Art director: Jonathan Hair
Design: Blue Paw Design
Picture research: Sophie Hartley
Consultants: Fiona M. Collins and Philippa Hunt,
Roehampton University

A CIP catalogue record for this book is available from the British Library.

ISBN: 978 0 7496 8658 1

Dewey Classification: 796.72

Acknowledgements:
Image courtesy of The Advertising Archives: 11b. © Gero Breloer/dpa/Corbis: 40. © Diego Azubel/epa/Corbis: 17. ©
Ferrari/epa/Corbis: 15t. © How Hwee Young/epa/Corbis: 34. © Michael Kim/Corbis: 39. © Juergen Tap/NewSport/Corbis: 6-7. ©
Schlegelmilch/Corbis: 8, 9, 13, 36-37 & 38. Goh Chai Hin/AFP/Getty Images: 7t. Stan Honda/AFP/Getty Images: 30-31. Josep
Lago/AFP/Getty Images: 16 & 32. Antonio Scorza/AFP/Getty Images: 41. AllsportUK/Getty Images: 18-19. Mike Powell/Allsport/Getty
Images: 19b. Fisher/Central Press/Getty Images: 10. Ferrari/Getty Images: 14-15. Paul Gilham/Getty Images: 21. Clive Mason/Getty
Images: Frontispiece, 33 & 35. Bob Thomas/Getty Images: 12b & 23. © iStockphoto.com/Andy Cook: 30-31 (insets). ©
iStockphoto.com/Kiyoshi Takahase Segundo: Endpapers. David Davies/PA Archive/PA Photos: Cover. photolibrary/Sutton Motorsport
Images: 12t. Alinari/TopFoto: 20. AP/TopFoto: 11t. National Motor Museum/HIP/TopFoto: 22.

Every attempt has been made to clear copyright. Should there be any
inadvertent omission please apply to the publisher for rectification.

Printed in China

Franklin Watts is a division of Hachette Children's Books,
an Hachette UK company.
www.hachette.co.uk

*Every effort has been made by the Publishers to ensure that the websites
in this book contain no inappropriate or offensive material. However,
because of the nature of the Internet, it is impossible to guarantee that the
contents of these sites will not be altered. We strongly advise that Internet
access is supervised by a responsible adult.*

Contents

Words that are highlighted can be found in the glossary.

What is Formula One?

Formula One is the highest class **of motor racing. It is also the fastest, the richest and the most popular.**

The word 'formula' stands for the rules the drivers and car **constructors** follow. The rules are very strict. They say how the car is made, how the driver races and even what he is allowed to wear.

There are two competitions in Formula One: the drivers' championship and the constructors' – or team – championship.

Felipe Massa drives his Ferrari out of the team garage.

? Do you watch Formula One racing on the television? What do you enjoy most about the racing?

Need for speed

Speed is one of the reasons Formula One is so popular. People have always liked to watch the fastest cars in the world racing against each other.

Around 55 million people watch each Formula One race on TV. The sport is loved worldwide, but it began in Europe. This is where most of its drivers, constructors and races were originally based.

Safety is important too. In the 1950s, 1960s and 1970s, a lot of Formula One drivers were killed in accidents. Today, the way the cars are made and the rules of the track make things as safe as possible.

GT Top Fact

This crash in 1970 involved Jackie Oliver's **BRM** and Jacky Ickx's Ferrari. Luckily, both drivers walked away with only minor injuries.

Jackie Stewart drives his March-Ford past the crash.

Formula One is now an international motorsport. Half the races take place away from Europe. Countries such as China and Bahrain have Formula One **Grand Prix** races today.

ONLINE//:

http://news.bbc.co.uk/sport1/hi/motorsport/formula_one /default.stm Website of BBC Sport, featuring Formula One videos, a circuit guide, race results, and a championship table

Racing history

Different cars have been racing in Formula One since 1954. Back then cars were very different.

? Look at the two racing cars on this page. What are the differences between them and the modern Formula One car on the cover of this book? What things are the same?

The 1950 Alfa Romeo (above) won the first Formula One championship, with the Italian driver Giuseppe Farina. Its engine was at the front of the car. The driver had no seatbelt and no special protection.

The 1959 Cooper was the first Formula One car to have its engine behind the driver. This made it easier to race at higher speeds. It was driven to victory in the 1959 (below) and 1960 championships by the Australian, Jack Brabham.

GT Top Fact

The 1959 Cooper was named after John Cooper who built it. He also helped **Morris** build their Mini Cooper in 1961.

IT'S WIZARDRY ON WHEELS!

The Revolutionary

MORRIS Mini-Minor

Later cars could travel even faster because of new aerodynamic designs.

The 1968 Lotus 49 was the first car to introduce aerodynamics. The rear wing pushed air up and the car down, so it could drive round corners more quickly.

Graham Hill in his Lotus 49B at the Mexican Grand Prix.

Ten years later, the 1978 Lotus 79 (below) was the first car to look like a modern Formula One car. It won the 1978 drivers' and constructors' championships.

In 1992, the Williams FW14B (below) became the first car to use computers to control many of its functions. But some people thought this made the cars too fast. As a result, some of the new functions were banned.

The 2004 Ferrari F2004 marked a new breed of racing car. It was driven by Michael Schumacher and won 15 of the 18 races in the 2004 season.

ONLINE//:

http://www.williamsf1.com
Website of the Williams Formula One racing team, including the team history, the latest car design, podcasts, videos and an image gallery.

Cars today

Today, cars are built to drive faster – and to be safer. Each part of the car has some role in making sure it performs at its best.

The Formula One car below is the Ferrari F2008. It shares many features with other Formula One cars.

Rear warning light

Survival cell

Engine

Fuel tank

Rear wing

Rear tyres

The steering wheel lets the driver control his car, **analyse** its performance, talk on the radio and even press a button to have a drink.

Air intakes

Front wing

ONLINE//:

http://news.bbc.co.uk/sport1/hi/motorsport/formula_one
/car_guide/default.stm

An interactive look at the different parts of a Formula One car.

The driver

Each team has two drivers. The driver's clothes are an essential part of his safety. There is more to them than just a set of overalls and a helmet.

Go Turbo Gear

- Helmet – protects the driver's head against impact. It is made of layers of plastic and **carbon fibre**.

- Visor – covered in several strips the driver can tear off, to get rid of dirt.

- Flame-proof balaclava worn under the helmet (see right).

- Flame-proof gloves and underwear.

- Boots with thin soles, so the driver can feel the pedals under his feet.

- Overalls made of multi-layered plastic that are flameproof, but also allow the skin to pass out sweat.

Nelson Piquet Jr and Fernando Alonso in their Renault team overalls.

GT Top Fact

Teams get 80% of their income from advertisements on the cars and the drivers' overalls and helmet. Why was tobacco advertising banned in 2006?

ONLINE//:

http://www.fernandoalonso.com
Official website of Fernando Alonso (click on the English version).
Features include: news archive, photo gallery and championship news.

Top drivers

The best drivers live to drive Formula One cars. Some have raced over 200 times. One driver, Juan Manuel Fangio, won nearly half the races he took part in.

Jackie Stewart in his BRM in 1967.

Go Turbo Winners

Eight drivers have won the Formula One championship three or more times. They are:

Name	Nationality	Championships won	Races raced in	Races won	Percentage of wins/race
Michael Schumacher	German	7	250	91	36%
Juan Manuel Fangio	Argentinian	5	51	23	45%
Alain Prost	French	4	200	51	26%
Jackie Stewart	British	3	100	27	27%
Ayrton Senna	Brazilian	3	162	41	25%
Nikki Lauda	Austrian	3	173	25	14%
Nelson Piquet	Brazilian	3	207	23	11%
Jack Brabham	Australian	3	126	14	11%

Alain Prost (left) and Nikki Lauda (right) in 1984.

Two drivers stand out as the best: Juan Manuel Fangio (below centre) and Michael Schumacher (right).

GT Top Fact

Juan Manuel Fangio won nearly half of his 51 races. He was 46 years old when he won his last championship in 1957.

In the 1950s, Juan Manuel Fangio won five of the first seven Formula One drivers' championships. He came second in the other two. Back then, Formula One cars were hard to handle and driving was very dangerous. In fact, while Fangio raced, 11 other drivers were killed in Formula One.

Michael Schumacher has won the most races and the most championships since Formula One began. He was the best driver in the sport for a decade, winning in 1994, 1995 and five times from 2000–2004.

GT Record

Michael Schumacher won more than a third of his 250 races.

The cars he drove were fast and safe. Throughout his **reign**, no other drivers were killed.

ONLINE//:

http://www.formula1.com/teams_and_drivers
Current championship drivers, including driver profiles, racing helmet designs and race videos (for private viewing only – see website)

Tragedies

Since Formula One began, 24 drivers have been killed, either during a race or during qualifying**.**

The first death was the Argentinian, Onofre Marimon, in 1954. He crashed during qualifying for the German Grand Prix.

GT Top Fact

The 1950s, 60s and 70s saw almost one death a year. But since 1982 only two drivers have lost their lives.

Marimon at the wheel of his Maserati in 1951.

? Why do you think the number of deaths during Formula One races has been reduced?

The last driver to die was probably the most famous driver of all. Ayrton Senna (above), was world champion in 1988, 1990 and 1991. He was killed in San Marino in 1994. His car went out of control at 310 kilometres per hour (kph) before he crashed into a safety barrier.

ONLINE//:

http://www.f1complete.com/content/category/17/221/521
Website featuring details of the latest Formula One safety equipment, including labelled cutaway illustrations.

Commentators' Curse

Written by Leon Read   Illustrated by Kevin Hopgood

Jon: Welcome to the closing stages of the Australian Grand Prix. It's been a real thriller so far, and I don't think these last few laps are going to be any different.

Barry: That's right Jon. The latest weather forecast is for rain any second now. I'm looking out of the commentary box window. Those dark black clouds certainly look stormy.

Jon: Too right. If it starts to rain now it could be a real problem. All the cars have dry tyres on. They'll be no good in the rain.

Barry: The teams will either bring their cars into the pits to get wet tyres, or hope they can make it round to the finish. Uh oh – there are spots of rain on the window, Jon.

Jon: Here comes the rain! And race leader Hamilton is pulling into the pits. He slides on the wet surface!

Barry: Hamilton gets the car back on the track. That's his first mistake today. But look, second-place Alonso is right behind him.

Jon: This could be a fight right to the finish line.

Barry: All the pit teams are ready. Into the pits come Hamilton and Alonso, with Hamilton just ahead. The clock is ticking. Off come the four dry tyres, on go the new wet tyres.

Jon: They'll give the cars a lot more grip. Just look at the rain pouring down, Barry.

Barry: Hamilton is away. Can he get out before Alonso, to stay in first place?

Jon: Yes! Yes, he can. Hamilton drives past Alonso just as he pulls out. That was a quick tyre change by Alonso's pit crew.

Barry: Here's third-place Massa.

Jon: Is Massa's engine sounding rough? What's that puff of smoke?

Barry: Massa's getting out! His engine is on fire!

Jon: The pit crew are quick on the scene.

Barry: The fire is out, but smoke is drifting across the pit lane.

Jon: We're into the last lap now. Hamilton is seconds away from taking his place on the winner's podium. His car has performed really well in these tough conditions.

Barry: Yes, Jon. Even with the heavy rain, he's had an almost perfect drive. What a dream finish this will be. And here he comes, heading into the final straight.

Jon: Hamilton's slowing down Barry.

Barry: Oh, I hope we haven't spoken too soon. Has he got a problem? My goodness! Hamilton's got a problem! His car is slowing down.

Jon: Through the rain I can just see second-place Alonso.

Barry: I can't believe it. Hamilton's going to lose the race in the last 20 metres. There's smoke! Smoke is pouring from Hamilton's engine.

Jon: Alonso moves out to overtake.

Barry: Alonso takes the chequered flag! Alonso wins the Australian Grand Prix!

Jon: Hamilton is furious. He's banging his hands on the steering wheel. You've got to feel sorry for him though.

Flags and the safety car

Safety on the track has dominated Formula One, especially in recent years. The way cars are designed is carefully monitored, sometimes to make them go slower.

If something dangerous happens on the track, one of the ways of telling the drivers is to use flags. Each flag means a different thing.

Oil on the track.

Warns a driver that another car is overtaking.

The driver must come into the pits – they have been **disqualified**.

There is an accident or **obstruction** on the circuit. Cars must slow down and not overtake each other.

The race is stopping because of severe danger.

Flag waved to the first car over the finish line, to show they have won.

Michael Schumacher wins the US Grand Prix in 2006.

Using a safety car is another way to make sure the circuit is safe during a race. The safety car drives at the front. It limits the speed of the cars when there has been an accident or there is an obstruction on the track.

GT *Top Fact*

The current safety car is based on the Mercedes SL 63 AMG. It has a 6.3 litre **V8** engine and can accelerate from 0 to 100 kph in 4.6 seconds. Why do you think the car needs to be so fast?

Once the safety car is on the track, the drivers cannot overtake.

The safety car drives in front of the car in first place. The other cars soon catch up. The safety car must still drive quickly, otherwise the sensitive Formula 1 engines would overheat and their tyres and brakes would cool down too much.

GT Top Fact

The driver of the safety car turns off its flashing yellow lights on the lap when it is due to pull in to re-start the race.

ONLINE//:

http://www.formula1.com/inside_f1/understanding _the_sport/5300.html Safety car webpage in this guide to understanding Formula One.

Racing circuits

There are more than 20 Grand Prix circuits used for Formula One racing. New tracks are sometimes introduced. In 2011 India will host a race for the first time.

Go Turbo Winners

These are the tracks that won a place in the 2009 Formula One calendar:

1. Melbourne, Australia
2. Kuala Lumpur, Malaysia
3. Shanghai, China
4. Sakhir, Bahrain
5. Catalunya, Spain
6. Monte Carlo, Monaco (on map)

This is the most famous street race in the world: the Monaco Grand Prix.

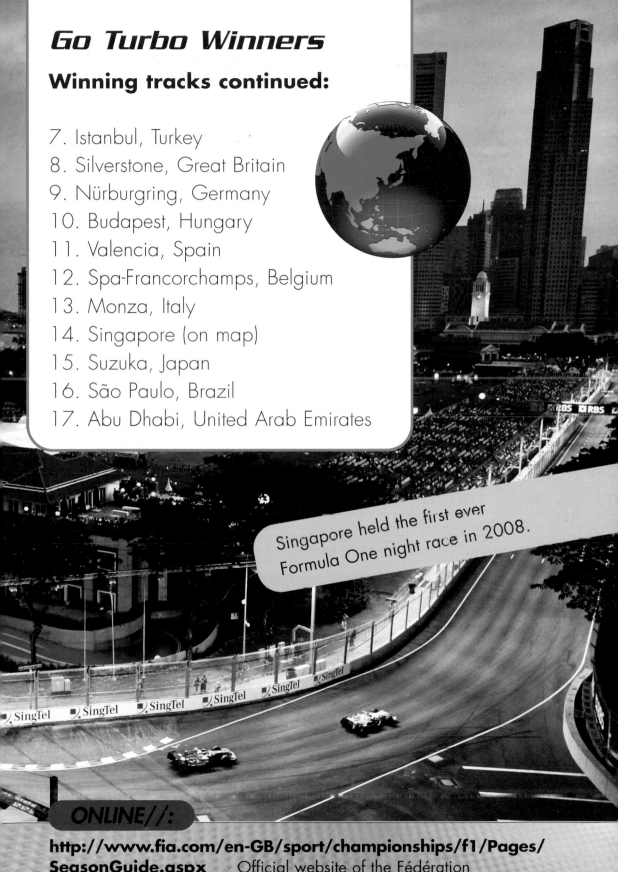

Go Turbo Winners

Winning tracks continued:

7. Istanbul, Turkey
8. Silverstone, Great Britain
9. Nürburgring, Germany
10. Budapest, Hungary
11. Valencia, Spain
12. Spa-Francorchamps, Belgium
13. Monza, Italy
14. Singapore (on map)
15. Suzuka, Japan
16. São Paulo, Brazil
17. Abu Dhabi, United Arab Emirates

Singapore held the first ever Formula One night race in 2008.

ONLINE//:

http://www.fia.com/en-GB/sport/championships/f1/Pages/ SeasonGuide.aspx   Official website of the Fédération Internationale de L'Automobile featuring all the Formula One circuits.

Pit stop

Formula One cars need new tyres during a race. They make a pit stop by driving into the pit lane. There the team is waiting, ready for action.

Mechanics remove worn tyres and replace them with new ones.

The pit team must make the pit stop as quickly as possible, so their driver does not lose too many places in the race.

A jack is used to lift the car off the ground.

Constructors

As well as the drivers' championship, the teams, or constructors, compete to see who has the best cars. Many teams have taken part since Formula One racing began.

Christian Horner watches the progress of his Red Bull team.

Each Formula One team has a boss who runs the team. Bosses watch the race with the rest of their senior team members on screens in their pit areas. They also monitor the performance of their cars.

Go Turbo Winners

These are the top four racing teams:

Team name	Country based in	Year formed	Constructors' championship wins
Ferrari	Italy	1950	16
Williams	Britain	1977	9
McLaren	Britain/Germany	1966	8
Renault	France	1977	2

Mechanics and **technicians** also make up part of the team.

Felipe Massa leads the way in his Ferrari.

Two of the biggest teams in Formula One today are Ferrari and McLaren.

Scuderia Ferrari (usually just called Ferrari) is the oldest team left in Formula One. It is also the most successful. It has 15 drivers' championships and 16 constructors' championship wins. Ferrari holds the record for the most race wins, too.

Ferrari has had some of the world's greatest racers drive its cars. The most famous and most successful was Michael Schumacher (raced 1991–2006).

McLaren have won the drivers' championship 12 times and the constructors' 8 times. McLaren cars are powered by Mercedes-Benz 2.4-litre engines.

GT Record

In 2008, McLaren driver Lewis Hamilton became the youngest man in history to win the championship. He was 23 years old.

ONLINE//:

http://www.ferrariworld.com/FWorld/fw/index.jsp
Official website featuring everything about the Ferrari racing team.
http://www.mclaren.co.uk   Official McLaren team website.

Fast facts

During a race the tyres can reach 130 degrees Celsius (C). Any hotter than that and the rubber would start to melt. The brake pads reach over 1,000 degrees C.

There are up to 5,000 parts in a Formula One car engine.

On average, a Formula One car accelerates from 0 to 100 kilometres per hour in 1.7 seconds.

Drivers have to control the car throughout the race, especially on corners. If the front wheels lose grip it is called understeer. If the back wheels lose grip it is called oversteer.

In 2008, South African driver Alan van der Merwe set an unofficial record for the fastest kilometre in a Formula One car at 415 kilometres per hour.

Answers

These are suggested answers to questions in this book. You may find that you have other answers. Talk about them with your friends. They may have other answers too.

Page 7: The answer to this question will depend on your own choices. If you watch perhaps you enjoy the fast cars, the roar of the engines or the crashes!

Page 10: The car on the cover is a McClaren. Things that are different compared to the cars on pages 10–11: it has wings (see page 12), thick tyres to help grip the track and the driver is better protected by the car. Things that are the same: they all have four wheels, a long smooth body and a driver in a central riding position.

Page 17: Tobacco advertising was banned because people didn't want smoking to be seen as glamorous, or to associate the sport with something that is unhealthy.

Page 23: The number of deaths has been reduced because greater efforts have been made to keep drivers safe in the cars and out on the circuits.

Page 32: The safety car needs to drive quickly enough to stay ahead of the very fast Formula One cars.

More websites

Official website of the Force India Formula One team, featuring an image gallery, team news and downloadables, including screensavers:

http://www.forceindia f1.com

Official website of the Toyota team, featuring a look behind the scenes at the team, image gallery, Toyota's motorsport history, plus a special 'how they built the car' webpage:

http://www.toyota-f1.com/en/index.html

Official website of the Red Bull Formula One team, includes race season updates, car information, an image gallery and news articles:

http://www.redbull racing.com

Official website of the BMW team, includes interactive race data, an image gallery, videos and team news:

http://www.bmw-sauber-f1.com/en

Official website of the Renault team, includes an image gallery, videos, podcasts and other goodies:

http://www.ing-renaultf1.com/en

Technical drawings of parts from the latest Formula One cars, including aerodynamic packages:

http://www.formula1.com/news/technical

Commercial motorsports website that features a Formula One archive, regulations and videos:

http://en.f1-live.com/f1/en/index.shtml

Glossary

Aerodynamic – a smooth shape that moves through the air easily.

Air intakes – open vents that direct air onto the car radiators which cool down the engine.

Analyse – to study something in detail.

BRM – British Racing Motors; a Formula One team that raced from 1955 to 1977. The team won 17 races.

Carbon fibre – a strong, flexible, lightweight material made from thin strands of carbon glued together.

Class – in motor racing, a group of cars of the same type that usually race together.

Constructors – in motor racing, the teams that build, maintain and race cars.

Disqualified – when a driver is removed from a race.

Grand Prix – a French word, it describes any race in the world championship.

Morris – a British car company that started in 1910. It built many famous cars, including the Mini Minor.

Obstruction – an object that is blocking the way. An obstruction on a circuit is usually a broken-down car, or a piece of car from a crash.

Qualifying – the period of time when drivers race to determine the final racing order. The car with the fastest time starts in pole position.

Reign – a period of time that someone is the leader, or at the top of their sport.

Survival cell – the specially designed cockpit in a Formula One car that protects a driver in a crash.

Technicians – members of a Formula One team who analyse and adjust the car's performance.

V8 – a powerful car engine that has 8 cylinders arranged in a 'V' shape.

Index